MINI HORSE

Ann Matzke

Rourke
Educational Media

rourkeeducationalmedia.com

Scan for Related Titles
and Teacher Resources

Before Reading:

Building Academic Vocabulary and Background Knowledge

Before reading a book, it is important to tap into what your child or students already know about the topic. This will help them develop their vocabulary, increase their reading comprehension, and make connections across the curriculum.

1. *Look at the cover of the book. What will this book be about?*
2. *What do you already know about the topic?*
3. *Let's study the Table of Contents. What will you learn about in the book's chapters?*
4. *What would you like to learn about this topic? Do you think you might learn about it from this book? Why or why not?*
5. *Use a reading journal to write about your knowledge of this topic. Record what you already know about the topic and what you hope to learn about the topic.*
6. *Read the book.*
7. *In your reading journal, record what you learned about the topic and your response to the book.*
8. *After reading the book complete the activities below.*

Content Area Vocabulary
Read the list. What do these words mean?

blind spots
breeders
companion
conformation
halter
paddock
pasture
stable
temperament
thrush
withers

After Reading:

Comprehension and Extension Activity

After reading the book, work on the following questions with your child or students in order to check their level of reading comprehension and content mastery.

1. *What does a mini horse need to feel safe and comfortable? (Summarize)*
2. *How does the way a horse sees affect how you approach it? (Infer)*
3. *In what ways is a mini horse similar to a cat or dog? How are they different? (Asking questions)*
4. *The text states mini horses were bred hundreds of years ago. Why do you think mini horses were bred? (Infer)*
5. *Would a mini horse be a good pet for you and your family? Explain. (Text to self connection)*

Extension Activity

The mini horse came to America in the 19th century. Why did Americans want a mini horse? Why do people have mini horses today? Research the mini horse's time in America. Create a visual timeline that shows how their purpose has changed from when they first arrived in America until today.

Table of Contents

A Horse of Course

Horses come in many colors and sizes. Miniature horses, called minis, are the smallest. They are less than half the size of a regular horse.

Horses are measured from the ground to their **withers**. Minis stand 24 to 34 inches (62 to 86 centimeters) high and weigh 150 to 250 pounds (68 to 113 kilograms).

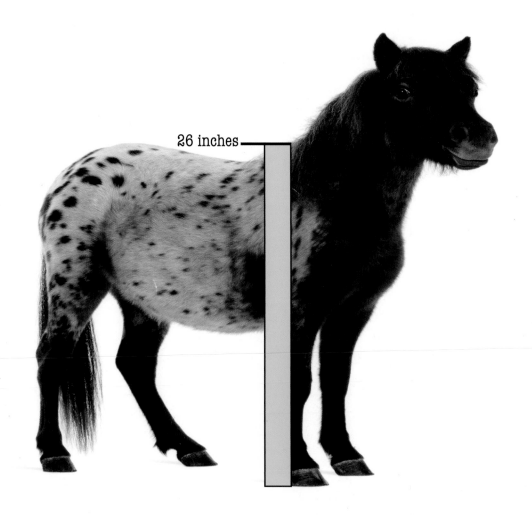

26 inches

The miniature horse size happened over a long period of time. For generations, **breeders** chose smaller and smaller horses to achieve the mini size.

In the 1500s, royal families in Europe kept minis as pets for princes and princesses. A mini makes a great pet because of its size and **temperament**.

 Some miniature horse shows have special competitions for children.

From Head to Tail

A horse's withers is the area on its back just after the neck but above the shoulders.

The hair between the horse's ears that falls onto the forehead is called the forelock.

The muzzle is the area of the horse's head that includes the mouth and nostrils.

Knowing the correct words for the different parts of a horse is an important part of owning and caring for a mini.

❮ The elbow-like joint of the horse's back legs are called hocks.

❮ The horse's ankle is called a fetlock.

Deciding on and buying a new pet is a big decision. Take plenty of time and look for a mini with good **conformation**, or physical appearance.

A mini should be well balanced, healthy, and free of physical problems that keep it from moving easily.

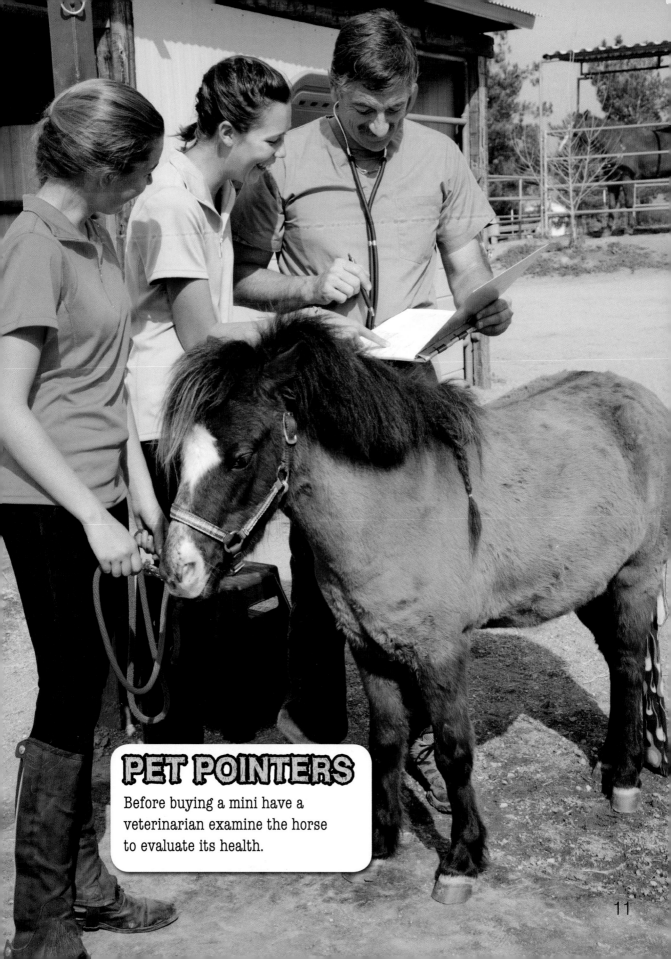

PET POINTERS

Before buying a mini have a
veterinarian examine the horse
to evaluate its health.

Horse Sense

Horses' ears swivel front to back so they can catch sounds in every direction, plus hear things in the distance.

They recognize you by how you smell. Hold out your hand first for a mini to sniff. Their sense of smell is exceptional; they can smell water and people in the distance.

Mini horses are known for showing gentle affection toward humans.

A mini horse sees separately out of each eye 340 degrees without moving its head. Each eye can focus on a different object at the same time. This wide view creates two **blind spots** for horses, one directly in front and the other right behind them.

Knowing how a horse sees can help you understand its behavior.

PET POINTERS

Always approach a horse from the side where it can see you.

Keeping and Caring for Minis

Make sure you can keep a miniature horse where you live. Zoning laws may have specific regulations or guidelines about stabling, or housing, minis.

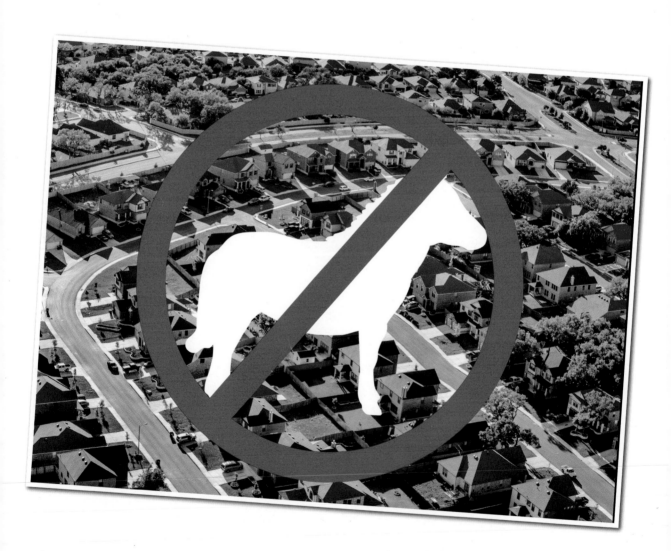

Minis, like full-size horses, require special care. It is important to record information either in a notebook or a card file, on a computer or on a smartphone app.

Track information on: visits to the vet, medications, worming schedules, immunizations, feed and hay management, **stable** maintenance, training schedules, and show records.

...e to a new home can be stressful. Horses a...
...o changes in their surroundings, other anim...
...and daily routines.
...your mini often and give it a good scratch c...
... a gentle rub on the side. This shows you c...
...ad your mini around its new home. You war...
...ed for and safe.

...people keep minis so children can learn to ride at an...

A box stall stable offers a mini horse protection from the Sun, weather, and insects. Make sure the stable has a secure latch, a high ceiling, good ventilation, a level dirt floor, and plenty of straw for bedding.

▶▶ *A mini horse kept in a stall should be given plenty of time to exercise and roam freely.*

Minis need space to roam. Make sure they have a secure, fenced **paddock**. Because of their smaller size, regular farm fencing may not work. They also need time in a **pasture** to graze.

▶▶ *Mini horses can be a variety of colors. Some are spotted. Some have patches. Some have tails and manes that are different colors.*

Grooming is an everyday routine. Currie, or rub, the mini horse's coat to loosen dirt and tangles. Use a brush to make the mini horse's coat lie flat, and a comb to smooth out its mane and tail.

Mini horses don't need horseshoes like full-size horses, but their hooves do require proper trimming and cleaning. Use a hoof pick to clean out hooves regularly. This prevents diseases such as **thrush**. Removing horse manure from a mini's stall can help prevent hoof problems.

PET POINTERS

Grooming tools you'll need: small size currycomb, body brush, hoof pick, finishing brush.

No Horsing Around

Be safe around your mini by understanding how they think. Plan ahead to avoid accidents.

Walking toward a mini, talk in a calm voice and stay where they can see you. Minis don't like surprises. Tell it your plan with a gentle touch on its neck or side.

Youth showmanship competitions allow children to show off their horse-handling skills.

FUN FACT

The American Miniature Horse Association was founded in 1978. It keeps track of mini horses all over the world.

Something's Up!
If a mini's ears are tipped forward and its head is high, that means it is interested in something. You'll see this when filling a mini's feedbox with hay.

It's Cool!
A relaxed horse will rest the toe of a back leg on the ground. Ears will be up and turned slightly to the side.

Frustrated
Swishing its tail when there are no flies around indicates frustration. It may also mean the mini's stomach hurts.

What's Going On?
When you can see the white part of its eyes and the ears are laid back flat, the mini may be scared, confused, or angry.

Rabbit Ears
Turning and twitching its ears in every direction means a mini is listening to something close or far away.

I'm Mad!
Lifting a back leg as if ready to kick indicates anger. The mini's ears are turned back, nostrils flared, and it may be showing teeth.

I Want Out
A mini pawing its front feet may want out of its enclosure. It can also mean the mini has a bellyache.

Just Horse Talk
Mini horses whinny to one another, nicker a friendly greeting when you approach, snort when they are unsure of something, blow, sigh, grunt, groan, and even scream when in pain.

Minis need special tack that fits their unique size. Tack is the equipment horses wear while being handled.

Always tie up your mini's **halter** while grooming it. This will remind it that it is not time to play. Keeping a regular routine helps a mini to understand.

Mini horses are the right size to take inside a nursing home, hospital, or a classroom.

Their gentle temperament and friendliness can cheer up children and adults. Therapy programs use minis with the sick and elderly. As guide or service horses, they make great **companion** animals for people with disabilities.

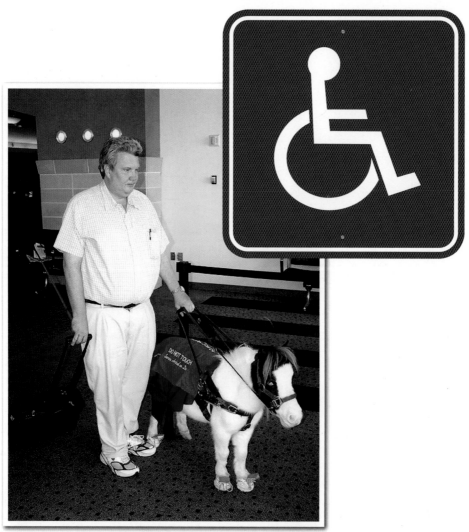

▶▶ *Guide minis help their owners get around safely. These service animals are housebroken like dogs.*

...use they are naturally curious and eager to please, ...e easy to train. They can learn to jump, pull a ...d compete in shows. There are many types of ...titions a mini and its owner can participate in.

A trained mini horse can easily pull a cart holding two adults fo...

These pint-size horses make wonderful pets. They will enjoy being with you as much as you'll enjoy being with them.

▶▶ *Mini horses grow a thick winter coat that helps keep them warm. They shed this coat in the spring.*

Things to Think About
If You Want a Pet Mini Horse

- Can you keep a mini where you live?
- Do you have the time for daily grooming and the time needed to care for a mini?
- Can you afford the expense involved with feeding and caring for a mini?
- Do you want a mini as a pet or do you want to show and compete with your mini?

Glossary

blind spots (blinde spahtz): the areas directly in front of and behind a horse where they have no vision

breeders (bree-DURS): people who breed horses

companion (KUHM-pan-yuhn): someone who helps another

conformation (kohn-fohr-MAY-shuhn): the shape and physical characteristics of a horse that allow them to move smoothly

halter (HAWL-tur): a piece of headgear worn by a horse for leading

paddock (PAD-uhk): an enclosed field or area where horses can graze or exercise

pasture (pas-TURE): land covered with grass for grazing animals

stable (STAY-buhl): a building or a part of a building where horses or cattle are kept

temperament (tem-pur-uh-muhnt): nature or personality; the way a person or animal behaves or responds to others or particular situations

thrush (THRUSH): a disease of the hoof from standing in a dirty stable that can cause serious problems with horses' hooves

withers (WITH-urs): the highest point of the horse's back, at the base of the neck between the shoulder blades

Index

Show What You Know

1. How do you measure the height of a mini?

2. How will a mini act when it is angry?

3. What is important to remember about approaching any horse?

4. What is special about a mini's sense of hearing and vision?

5. Name two things that are important to know before owning a mini.

Websites to Visit

www.sciencekids.co.nz/sciencefacts/animals/horse.html

www.horses.animal-world.com/Light-Horse-Breeds/MiniatureHorse.php

www.theminiaturehorse.com/ministoday.html

About the Author

Ann H. Matzke is a children's librarian. She has an MFA in Writing for children and young adults from Hamline University. She grew up having many different kinds of pets: cats, fish, turtles, hamsters, gerbils, and fire-bellied toads. Ann and her family live in Gothenburg, Nebraska with their chocolate lab, Penny and three cats, Max, Michael, and Bean. Ann enjoys traveling, reading, and writing books for children.

Meet The Author!
www.meetREMauthors.com

© 2016 Rourke Educational Media

www.rourkeeducationalmedia.com

PHOTO CREDITS: Cover: ©Rhea Magaro; page 1, page 7: ©Andrew N Dierks; page 3: ©24Novembers; page 4: ©lifeonwhite; page 5 (top): ©Asian Alphan; page 5 (middle): ©AlonzoDesign; page 5 (bottom), page 14: ©Stefania Hill; page 6: ©horseman; page 8: ©Eriklam; page 9: ©Bedrin; page 10: ©vonne Wierink; page 11: ©Alina Solovyova-Vincent; page 12, page 22: ©Geoffrey Kuchera; page 13: ©Abramova Kseniya; page 14: ©David Sucsy; page 15: ©Mehmet Ozcan; page 16: ©Vcarmstrong; page 17: ©artazum; page 18: ©Chalyaphong Kitphaephaisan; page 19 (left): ©Charles Mann; page 19 (right bottom): ©Eileen Groome; page 19 (right top): ©Van Brunschot; page 20 (right), page 27 (bottom): ©DaCek; page 20 (left): ©Stefanina Hill; page 21: ©Leszek Glasner; page 24-25: ©Porwas Tha; page 26 (right): ©KeithBishop; page 26 (left): ©wiki; page 27 (top) ©SkyF; page 28: ©Julia Kuznetsova; page 29: ©catnap72; page 30: ©Wimage72

Edited by: Keli Sipperley

Cover design and Interior design by: Rhea Magaro

Library of Congress PCN Data

Mini Horse/Ann Matzke
(You Have a Pet What?!)
ISBN 978-1-63430-434-4 (hard cover)
ISBN 978-1-63430-534-1 (soft cover)
ISBN 978-1-63430-623-2 (e-Book)
Library of Congress Control Number: 2015931857

Printed in the United States of America, North Mankato, Minnesota

Also Available as: